WITHDRAWN

FRANKLIN PARK PUBLIC LIBRARY
FRANKLIN PARK, ILL.

Each borrower is held responsible for all library material drawn on his card and for fines accruing on the same. No material will be issued until such fine has been paid.

All injuries to library material beyond reasonable wear and all losses shall be made good to the satisfaction of the Librarian.

Replacement costs will be billed after 42 days overdue.

Bruce Hale

An Author Kids Love

Titles in the
Authors Kids Love Series

Alma Flor Ada

ISBN-13: 978-0-7660-2760-2
ISBN-10: 0-7660-2760-0

Bruce Coville

ISBN-13: 978-0-7660-2755-8
ISBN-10: 0-7660-2755-4

Bruce Hale

ISBN-13: 978-0-7660-2758-9
ISBN-10: 0-7660-2758-9

Jack Gantos

ISBN-13: 978-0-7660-2756-5
ISBN-10: 0-7660-2756-2

Bruce Hale

Authors
Kids Love

An Author Kids Love

by Michelle Parker-Rock

Enslow Elementary
an imprint of

Enslow Publishers, Inc.
40 Industrial Road
Box 398
Berkeley Heights, NJ 07922
USA

http://www.enslow.com

This book is based on a live interview with Bruce Hale on February 22, 2006, and includes photos from his collection.

For Larry, who has a serious thing for lizards, and for Rose J., who has a serious thing for classic films. And to B.H., aloha, namaste, and thanks.

Library of Congress Cataloging-in-Publication Data

Parker-Rock, Michelle.
    Bruce Hale : an author kids love / Michelle Parker-Rock.
        p. cm. — (Authors kids love)
    "Based on a live interview with Bruce Hale on February 22, 2006"—T.p. verso.
    Summary: "Discusses the life of children's author Bruce Hale, including his works of fiction, how he got into writing, and his tips for aspiring young writers"—Provided by publisher.
    Includes index.
    ISBN-13: 978-0-7660-2758-9
    ISBN-10: 0-7660-2758-9
    1. Hale, Bruce—Juvenile literature. 2. Authors, American—20th century—Biography—Juvenile literature. 3. Hale, Bruce—Interviews—Juvenile literature. 4. Authors, American—20th century—Interviews—Juvenile literature. 5. Children's stories—Authorship—Juvenile literature. I. Title.
    PS3558.A35625Z8 2008
    813'.54—dc22
    [B]
                                    2007029319

Printed in the United States of America

10 9 8 7 6 5 4 3 2 1

To Our Readers: We have done our best to make sure that all Internet Addresses in this book were active and appropriate when we went to press. However, the author and publisher have no control over and assume no liability for the material available on those Internet sites or on other Web sites they may link to. Any comments or suggestions can be sent by e-mail to comments@enslow.com or to the address on the back cover.

Photo Credits: Bruce Hale, pp. 5, 6, 15, 16, 20, 25, 26, 28, 29, 32, 41, 47, back cover; Michelle Parker-Rock © 2006, pp. 3, 5, 35, 39, 42; Shutterstock, pp. 5, 8, 12.

Cover Photo: Michelle Parker-Rock © 2006.

Contents

The Hitchhiking Lizard

"I was driving along the Pali Highway in Hawaii on my way home from working at the phone company," said popular children's book author Bruce Hale, "and I saw this flash of movement." He went on:

I looked forward, and there, with his feet glued to the car, was this little brown gecko. He was blowing in the wind, but he was hanging on. As I was driving around the corners, I kept my eye on him because I thought he was going to blow off. He never did. He had the strongest grip. He was like a hood ornament. He looked so noble.

Geckos

House geckos are quite common in Hawaii. They have suction cup-like toes that make it possible for them to cling to smooth surfaces like the hood of Hale's car. If caught by the tail, a gecko can detach it, scamper away, and grow a new one.

Bruce Hale

I thought he would be a good character and something fun to draw.

It was 1987, and Bruce Hale was living in Honolulu, Hawaii. He was working for GTE Hawaiian Tel, the local telephone company, writing newsletters for employees and hosting the company's video news magazine. That year, Hale and his girlfriend, Susana Brown, wanted to make homemade gifts for Christmas. Geckos are very common in Hawaii, and Hale and Brown thought that stuffed gecko toys would make good presents.

"My girlfriend was good with sewing, and since I was good at art, I did the design. We came up with these

8

little gecko stuffed toys, and we gave them to our friends."

It was not long before people wanted to buy the toys, so Hale and Brown started a small business making stuffed geckos, turtles, and other Hawaiian animals. The business did well, and Hale thought it would be fun to have a companion book to go with the gecko toys.

In Hawaii, the gecko is considered to be good luck, and Hale thought it would be a fine idea for a story. "It was just a common belief, but nobody had written about it," he said. Hale came up with an original idea that featured a character named Moki, a Hawaiian gecko.

When Hale started to work on the illustrations, he remembered his experience with the gecko on his car. "That really captured my attention," he said, "and it brought the gecko character to my imagination very clearly."

It took Hale more than a year and a half to complete the book, which he titled *The Legend of the Laughing Gecko*. "During some of that time, I'd work on it and think it was a terrible idea. I would toss it aside and do nothing for a few months and then come back to it."

Finally, Hale turned his attention to getting the book published. Although it was a business he knew nothing about, he had a stroke of luck. Inspired by the little gecko on his car, Hale was on his way to good fortune as a children's book author.

Moki

Hale and Brown decided to publish *The Legend of the Laughing Gecko* by themselves. This meant they had to raise the money for printing, rather than have a publishing company do it. They put an ad in the newspaper, seeking people who would put in some of their own money in hopes of making a profit on the book sales. Once they raised enough funds, they hired a person who arranged to have the book printed. In 1989, *The Legend of the Laughing Gecko* was ready for sale.

While Hale and Brown had had success marketing their toys by going from store to store, Hale realized that selling books required a different approach. "You have to have distribution," he said. Hale and Brown found a distributor who agreed to supply Hawaii's booksellers with their book.

Hale was amazed when he saw the book in the bookstore. "It was such a joy. I reconnected with my childhood self and the pleasure of creating my first little cardboard book," said Hale, referring to "The Two Brothers of Monster Town," a story he wrote in third grade. "It was mostly just drawings with a title on the front. The cover was cardboard and the inside was standard paper."

In Hawaii, the gecko is thought to be good luck.

Just as *The Legend of the Laughing Gecko* arrived in the stores, Hale's office job came to an end.

> During that same week, I won several awards for my newsletter writing. I went into the office and my boss said he wanted to talk to me. The good news was that I was getting a raise, but the bad news was that I only had two months to enjoy it because I was being laid off. So I took a very long early lunch and I walked around in a daze. That's when I saw my book for the first time in the bookshop, and I realized I had come to a crossroads.

Hale's boss offered to give him another job with the company somewhere on the United States mainland, but he did not want to go.

> I didn't want to leave Hawaii. I thought that I would just explore this whole world of children's books. I had done one book, so I'd do another and see where it took me. Being laid off was the boot out of the nest that I needed to actually work harder on my new career and my writing.

At the time, Hale did not realize that he had found a market that specialized in a unique product. "If you find your niche, you're very

Hale the Explorer

In 1979, Bruce Hale graduated from the University of California in Los Angeles, where he studied economics. His first job was selling Scotch tape over the telephone. Then he and a friend took off to work as oil explorers in Utah, Texas, Oklahoma, and Japan. Hale thought Japan was exciting. In 1983, he moved to Hawaii and took a job writing stories about air-conditioning systems for a trade magazine. That's where he learned how to edit his own writing. Hale worked there for about three years. Then in 1986, he went to work for GTE Hawaiian Tel.

fortunate," he said. "We were sitting right in the middle of a great fat niche. People who live in Hawaii love to buy books about Hawaii, and people who visit Hawaii love the same thing." *The Legend of the Laughing Gecko* was a Hawaiian-themed book, and it was the first book of its kind to come out. "At the time, it filled a need and people loved it," he said.

With the success of the first book, Hale tried his hand at another, this time without his friend and coauthor, Susana Brown. *Surf Gecko to the Rescue* also featured Moki, and the story focused on the importance of taking care of the environment. Hale is an

14

A beach in Honolulu, Hawaii. Hale moved
to Hawaii in 1983.

enthusiastic environmentalist. "I've been into body boarding and surfing since the late 1980s," he said. *Surf Gecko to the Rescue* came about when he saw that a beach he visited frequently was becoming polluted. "I loved going there, and so it really bothered me. Aside from cleaning it up, I wanted to do something. One of the things I did was write that story."

Even after two books, Hale didn't think of

Bruce Hale loves beaches and surfing. His concern for polluted beaches was the inspiration for *Surf Gecko to the Rescue.*

himself as a real children's author. The voice in his head said, "You know, you still haven't been accepted by a national publisher, so you're not legit. You just printed these on your own."

On the other hand, Hale was becoming very popular with the kids in Hawaii. He was frequently invited to schools to talk to the students. At one of his presentations, a young reader gave him the idea for another Moki adventure, which Hale entitled *Moki and the Magic Surfboard*.

Even though Hale's books were selling well in Hawaii and he was popular with young readers there, he wanted to be distributed nationally. He had written five Moki books in all, but he never submitted any of them to a big publishing house. "The Moki series was more a matter of fun," he said. "I had a niche, and it was successful, so I just kept doing it."

While working on the Moki series, Hale did freelance writing for various businesses, and he acted in commercials. He and a friend had also written a musical version of *The Legend of the Laughing Gecko*, and Hale was performing the show at schools in Hawaii. In addition, he continued to write stories and submit them to national publishers.

"I definitely saw myself as a writer," he said, "but I always wanted to publish nationally to reach a wider audience of readers."

Hale wrote a story called *Pony in the Kitchen* that was very similar to the *The Cat in the Hat*, although it did not occur to him how much alike they were at the time.

> I sent that out to at least thirty or forty publishers and everybody rejected it with a form letter. I thought, these people don't see genius when it's right in front of them. What is wrong with them? I was really disappointed. There was this sense that maybe they just don't get how good this story is.

Looking back at it now, Hale realizes that he was not a good judge of his own writing. Fortunately, he did not give up. He spent time learning his craft, and his work got progressively better. Before long, he had another stroke of luck. This time it was a gecko named Chet.

Chet

In 1997, Hale attended a writer's conference where he heard about editors who were looking for middle-grade mysteries and humorous stories. "I love reading detective fiction and thought I'd try my hand at writing a funny one," he said. However, he did not want his new main character to be another gecko. "I wanted to make my detective something different, like a dog or a cat," he said. Then one day while he was quickly jotting down ideas, a character's voice emerged, and Hale wrote:

> Kids talk. They say I'm someone who can solve mysteries. They're right. I can. Who am I? Chet Gecko, Private Eye.

Bruce with a drawing of Chet Gecko, his best-known character. Hale does the inside art for the Chet Gecko books himself.

"The name was perfect," said Hale, "and when I wrote it, I knew the gecko would not be denied."

Hale used those lines in the opening of *The Chameleon Wore Chartreuse*, the first Chet Gecko whodunit.

"I didn't know a thing about plotting a mystery, so most of my clues were in the form of riddles for Chet to solve," he said.

Hale sent the manuscript out to numerous publishing houses in October 1997. It was rejected twelve times in the next year. Finally, he got a note from a publisher saying they liked it and asking if he would do a rewrite.

Hale credits his later success to his ability to learn from his mistakes. "It would not have been possible if I didn't learn by doing all the wrong things," he said.

One realization Hale had was that most of the manuscripts he had submitted to national publishers were stories that he thought would make good books, but they were not based on things he felt passionate about.

To change that, he started writing from his heart. He said:

> I gave myself permission to be as goofy as I wanted to with the humor. I wrote about things that I loved. I loved film noir and detective stories. I think that the passion made a difference in the quality of my writing.

The initial draft of the first Chet Gecko manuscript was about twenty pages long. The final draft was about fifty-five pages. Hale's editor told him that more things needed to happen in the story and that the reader needed different kinds of clues. With each rewrite, the story got better. "I was learning how to write a mystery with that first book."

Then in 1998, Hale was awarded a Fulbright

Film Noir

Film noir was a popular type of movie in the 1940s and 1950s. The movies, filmed in black and white, were often mysteries that featured detectives or private eyes who had a crime to solve. The titles of the Chet Gecko books are a mix of classic film noir titles and Hale's clever humor. *The Big Nap* is a takeoff on a movie entitled *The Big Sleep*; *The Malted Falcon* is a takeoff on *The Maltese Falcon*; and *Murder, My Tweet* is a takeoff on *Murder, My Sweet*, to name a few.

Bruce Hale

grant, a sum of money given to him by the government to teach storytelling and to study folk stories in Thailand. When he returned to the United States, he met an agent at another writers' conference, and within three months, he signed a contract for three books. The contract was Hale's bridge to becoming a full-time children's book author.

"I did a black-and-white illustration of Chet Gecko to send along with the first story," he said. Chet loves to eat, so Hale made him chubby. The publisher liked it, so they said that he could do the inside art. However, they wanted someone else to do the covers in a different style. "It wasn't something that I could do," said Hale. "At first I was not real pleased about somebody else doing my covers, but after I saw them, I was very happy."

Hale believes that his readers identify with Chet Gecko.

> He's a little bit of a sarcastic guy, and he's a bit of a troublemaker. He also has a good sense of humor. Chet has his faults, but he has his strengths, too. He is very persistent, and he achieves what he sets out to do. I think kids enjoy that.

While there is a part of Hale that is like Moki, innocent and sweet, Hale thinks there is a bigger part of him that is like Chet. Chet has Hale's sense of humor, his curiosity, and his interest in solving mysteries.

"There's probably more of me in Chet than in any other character I've written so far," he said. "I'm not quite as much of a hog as Chet, but I do enjoy a chocolate chip cookie every now and then. I just don't go overboard like he does."

Chapter 4

Kid Writer

"When I was a kid, we lived in a suburb of Los Angeles called Palos Verdes Estates," said Hale. "It was a quiet place with lots of green hills. My mom and stepdad would let me go off and do my thing." Hale and his friend, whose nickname was Billy-the-Kid, would go rambling into the hills. He said:

> We'd get a little chunk of sourdough from my mom who loved to bake, and we'd just go and have adventures all day. We'd find tortoises and foxes and explore the storm drains to see where they led. It was great fun.

Halloween was one of Hale's favorite times of the year. "I would get inspired by a movie, a TV

24

series, or a book, and be that character," he said. "I really developed a love of costumes and hats."

Bruce at around age three with his mother, Ann.

However, until third grade, Hale was not very interested in books. Then one day, the family's TV broke, and his parents did not get it fixed right away. They started reading to him, but Hale did not enjoy it much at first. "I liked running around and causing trouble," he said.

I wasn't into sitting still and listening to stories. But then my stepdad got tired of reading children's books, and he pulled down one of his favorites from the shelf, which happened to be *Tarzan of the Apes*, by Edgar Rice Burroughs. That book just totally captured my imagination. I loved it. I got my mom to make me a little leopard skin loincloth. Then I climbed trees and swung around for quite awhile."

He remembers thinking, "If this is what books are about, then I love them."

Bruce Hale

As a boy, Bruce loved animals. He also enjoyed dressing up in costumes and pretending to be different characters.

At the same time, Hale discovered what an author is, and it was the first time that he thought that he might like to be a writer. But he was young, and he had other dreams as well.

"We went on 'Pirates of the Caribbean' at Disneyland, so I wanted to be a pirate," he said. He got a pirate hat and costume. Then he saw a movie called *Spartacus*, about ancient Rome, and he wanted to be a gladiator with a shield, a helmet, and a sword. In third grade, it was Tarzan, and around fourth grade, it was Daniel Boone. Hale also remembers wanting to be a fireman.

Although Hale does not recall saying that he wanted to be an author at such a young age, his friend Billy thought he heard him express an interest when they were back in grade school. "What I remember more," said Hale, "was wanting to be a cartoonist. That lasted through middle school, high school, and even into college."

As a young boy, Hale was not very athletic. "Billy-the-Kid and I tossed a football around, and we played a little Frisbee, but I didn't get into sports for fun until college and afterward."

Once Hale got into the world of reading, he and Billy traded books back and forth. "We read *The Hobbit* and *Lord of the Rings*, and we'd go out into the marshy area and pretend it was Mordor or something like that," said Hale.

"I didn't get the whole concept of homework initially," he said. "I thought it was optional." His teachers would give him assignments, and he would put them in the back of his desk and never look at them again. "I thought if you just put it away, no one would know. I got away with it probably up until third grade." Then his teacher and his parents talked with each other. "They busted me," he said. "That's when things started to change, and my parents impressed upon me the importance of studying. Now that I think about it, it came at the same time that I got into reading." As a result, his

Bruce climbing a tree at age seven with Billy-the-Kid. The two boys had lots of adventures.

28

studies improved from third grade on. "I was pretty much a straight A student in later middle school and high school," he said.

Billy-the-Kid and I used to love to make books together. We'd go up into my room and get a stack of cardboard, paper, and crayons and draw all afternoon and tape things together and go show everybody how cool we were to make books.

The little cardboard book, "The Two Brothers of Monster Town," that Hale created in third grade coincided with his discovery of the Tarzan stories.

In fourth grade, Hale was in a reading contest.

I was one of the winners of the contest. We got to go to the district headquarters and pick out the books the whole class was

Hale's college graduation photo. Once he figured out that he had to do his homework, Hale was a good student.

going to read. I thought this was pretty cool. It was a privilege. Plus we got a huge Nestle Crunch bar. Not to be sneezed at.

Hale loved to draw. In fifth grade, he became interested in making picture books and using word and thought balloons. "I really got into comics when I was in late elementary school and middle school," he said. *Fantastic Four*, *Superman*, and *Spiderman* were his favorites.

The Writer Guy

Hale lives in Santa Barbara, California, with his wife, Janette Cross. They met in an Afro-Caribbean dance class and were married in 1993. "We were sweating it up dancing," he said, "and we had a nice connection."

Hale loves to dance. He also loves to sing and play music. A few years ago, he played guitar in a band of children's authors called the Savage Bunnies. He sings with a jazz group that does musical performances and workshops for kids.

Hale writes at home. He starts his day with some exercise. He hikes, bikes, swims, or does yoga. Then he answers his e-mails.

Bruce and Janette were married in 1993.

He said:

In the afternoon, right after lunch, I'll start writing. Initially it's just brainstorming. Usually I'll brainstorm a book for at least a couple of weeks. Once I get past the brainstorming stage, I plunge into the first draft and write about four or five hours a day.

When Hale writes the Chet Gecko books, he sometimes starts with just a title and a descriptive paragraph. Then he asks himself questions about the story. When he was writing *The Big Nap*, he wondered whether the story should be about people being hypnotized or about people turning into mindless zombies. He decided on the latter. Then he had to come up with a way for Chet to realize what was happening and a way for him to figure out the clues.

Hale enjoys discovering things about a story as he writes it. He does a quick first draft that he edits lightly as he goes along. In the second, third, and fourth drafts, he gets into the heavy editing.

At the end of a day, Hale might leave a sentence unfinished on purpose. Then when he sits down the next day to write, he picks up where he left off the day before. He already knows how it is going to end, so he types the rest of the sentence, and he is ready to write. Sometimes he uses rewards to motivate himself. "It could be something like a walk on the beach or a massive chocolate chip cookie," he said.

As long as he and the readers are having fun with the Chet Gecko books, Hale will continue to write them. The series is popular with both boys and girls. "In the schools, the boys are the most passionate ones," said Hale, "but there seem to be just as many girls who love it." In fact, he said, "I get more e-mail from girls than I do from boys." Hale said that the books are for kids, but there is humor in the stories for adults, too.

Hale recently finished several new books. *Snoring Beauty* is a fairy-tale spoof. *Prince of Underwhere* and *Pirates of Underwhere* are the first books in a new series about three kids and a cat who fall through a hole and discover a strange world filled with zombies, little dinosaurs, and an evil warlord. He is currently working on a new

Hale Hails Hats

Hale has a hat rack dripping with hats. "I love wearing different hats," he said. "It's like playing different characters." He has several fedoras, two fezzes, a pork pie hat, and a half dozen berets. Hale does not wear hats just for style. He wears them to keep his head from being exposed to the sun. "I have little bare spaces up there, and at night it's cold. I want to have something warm on my head." Sometimes he sleeps with a wool cap. "When I go for a walk in the neighborhood," he said, "I'll wear a baseball cap." What about a shower cap? "I do not wear a shower cap. I draw the line. No shower cap."

Hale, wearing a pork pie hat, shows off the rest of his hat collection.

35

Chet Gecko book, *From Russia With Lunch*, and the third book in the Underwhere series, *Flyboy of Underwhere*.

Hale would like to be telling stories for the rest of his life. Whether he is telling a tale, writing a book or a screenplay, drawing illustrations, or singing a song, Hale believes they are all just different forms of storytelling. "Story is what fascinates me," he said. "Story is what I love."

Award-Winning Books

Bruce Hales's books have won many awards. Here are just a few of them:

The Chameleon Wore Chartreuse
- *Working Mother* magazine's "Favorite Books of 2000"
- Pennsylvania School Librarians' Association Readers Choice nominee, 2004–2005

This Gum for Hire
- Association of Booksellers for Children's Choice Award, 2002

The Malted Falcon
- Edgar Award finalist, Mystery Writers of America, 2004

Murder, My Tweet
- Little d award winner, Children's Literature Connection, 2005
- International Reading Association–Children's Book Council Children's Choice for Best Books of 2005

The Mystery of Mr. Nice
- *Working Mother* magazine's "Favorite Books of 2000"

Writerly Advice

$\mathcal{H}$ale often gives suggestions to young people who want to be writers. He said:

Many authors will tell you that the best advice is write, write, write, and read, read, read. They're right, but here's another tip that may help while you're writing. When you first write something, don't edit yourself and don't judge yourself in any way. Just throw the words on the page, and believe that they are all genius. I call this being in your "artist mind." On your first draft, write as quickly, loosely, and sloppily as possible. Then let your story cool off for a day, for two days, or for a week. At that point, get into your "editor mind"; think critically.

Hale also advises young writers to reread their work and ask the tough questions: Does this make sense? Will anyone want to read it? Is that word spelled properly? Did I leave something out?

He believes that writers must be good learners. He said an important aspect of being a writer is to continually challenge yourself and to try things you

Hale at work at his desk.

On Becoming a Writer

Bruce said:

There was this one kid in California who sent me an e-mail that said: "I was really inspired by your talk and I thought I would want to be an author. It sounds like a cool thing to do. But my friends tell me authors are bozos. I don't know what to do. Should I go play with them or should I follow my dream?" I was just really touched that a kid would confide in me in that way and ask for my opinion. I told him to follow his dream, because that is what I want to encourage kids to do. I wish people had told me that when I was a kid.

don't know you can do. "Even if you fail," he said, "you learn something."

One thing Hale learned is perseverance. This means he kept on trying even though he collected lots of rejection letters and it took him a long time to get published. He said:

I think the other thing that long detour taught me was to listen to my heart and listen to my dreams. When I was a kid, I wanted to be an illustrator, but I thought I couldn't do that for one reason or another. I spent a long time doing other things and not being happy. Sometimes you have to try the other stuff before you find out what you love.

Hale's goal is to contribute more positivity to the world, and he wants to inspire others through his children's books and when he speaks at schools, libraries, and conferences. He hopes to bring light into people's lives. The light could be in the form of a story, laughter, inspiration, or anything else. "Humor is just one of the gifts I was given," he said. "I love humor, and I love jokes, and I have a talent to be able to write those things."

Hale believes that all of his life's experiences have helped to shape him and that those experiences are expressed in his writing and drawing. He hopes he can help others see what they can do to follow

Bruce Hale in another hat from his collection.

49

Hale poses with a fan who has just bought one of his Chet Gecko books.

their own dreams. "If they see my life," he said, "and all the mistakes I've made, but they can still see how I manage to find a way to do what I love to do, then maybe that can inspire them to do the same. That's a gift."

Books by Bruce Hale

Picture Books
The Legend of the Laughing Gecko
How the Gecko Lost His Tail
Surf Gecko to the Rescue
Moki the Gecko's Best Christmas Ever
Moki and the Magic Surfboard
Snoring Beauty

Chet Gecko Mystery Series
The Chameleon Wore Chartreuse
The Mystery of Mr. Nice
Farewell, My Lunchbag
The Big Nap
The Hamster of the Baskervilles
This Gum for Hire
The Malted Falcon
Trouble Is My Beeswax
Give My Regrets to Broadway
Murder, My Tweet
The Possum Always Rings Twice
Key Lardo
Chet Gecko's Detective Handbook (and Cookbook)
Hiss Me Deadly

The Underwhere Series
Prince of Underwhere
Pirates of Underwhere

43

advance—Money given to an author before the book is finished.

brainstorming—Coming up with ideas for a plan or a project.

distributor—Somebody who provides a product to others.

economics—The study of the making, buying, selling, and using of goods and services.

editor—The person who is in charge of the publication of a book.

fedora (fuh-DOH-ra)—A soft hat with a rim around its edge and a long crease on top.

fez—A hat that is shaped like a cone with a flat top, no brim, and a tassel.

film noir (NWAHR)—A type of movie from the 1940s and 1950s.

laid off—Let go from a job.

mainland—The main part of a country's land (as opposed to an island off its coast).

niche (NITCH or NEESH)—A market that focuses on a specific product.

persistent—Determined.

pork pie hat—A man's hat with a flat top and a turned-up brim.

positivity—Hopefulness.

publisher—A person or a company that is in the business of editing, printing, and selling books.

trade magazine—A magazine for people in a specific business.

whodunit—A mystery book or movie.

45

Further Reading

Hale, Bruce. *Chet Gecko's Detective Handbook (and Cookbook): Tips for Private Eyes and Snack Food Lovers*. Orlando, Fla.: Harcourt, 2005.

Heinrichs, Ann. *Hawai'i*. Minneapolis: Compass Point Books, 2004.

Velthaus, Sally. *Geckos*. Mankato, Minn.: Capstone Press, 2006.

Official Bruce Hale Web site
<http://www.brucehale.com/>

Harcourt Authors: Bruce Hale
<http://www.harcourtbooks.com/booksearch/search_
  results.asp?sf=author&tp=simple&st=title&pg=
  1&q=Bruce%20Hale>

Bruce Hale: Speaker—Author—
Storyteller
<http://www.brucetalks.com>

Index